MW00860560

New Directions™ For Str
A Comprehensive String Method

JOANNE ERWIN • KATHLEEN HORVATH
ROBERT D. McCASHIN • BRENDA MITCHELL

WITH SUPPLEMENTAL ENSEMBLE MUSIC BY
ELLIOT DEL BORGO AND SOON HEE NEWBOLD

The Story of the DOUBLE BASS

The **double bass** is the lowest pitched string instrument in the orchestra. It has evolved greatly throughout history and is actually a combination of two different instruments called the *viol da bracchio* and the *viol da gamba*. It is the least standard of all of the stringed instruments. The double bass has had as few as three strings or as many as six; large or small shoulders; a round or flat back; can be played standing or sitting, and has a choice of two different bows. The double bass is the most unique of all the stringed instruments because it is so versatile. It has a notable history performing in the symphony orchestra, opera, wind ensemble, jazz band, chamber group, and even rock 'n roll. Some famous players in history have been Giovanni Bottesini, Domenico Dragonetti, Gary Karr, Ron Carter, Rufus Reid, and Edgar Meyer.

Care and Maintenance of Your Double Bass

It is very important that you care for your instrument as a valuable possession.
Here are important guidelines for the care of your instrument:

- loosen the hair on the bow when not playing so the stick does not warp

- make sure you take the bow out of the case first and put it in last

- rosin the bow with a few swipes each day you practice

- clean all rosin dust from the surfaces of the instrument, strings, and bow stick with a clean, soft cloth

- make sure the endpin is in and securely tightened anytime you are not playing the instrument

- protect your instrument from extreme temperatures and excessive moisture by keeping it in the case

You should take your instrument to a string repair specialist for a check up and have your strings replaced and bow rehaired at least once a year. A well-maintained instrument can last literally hundreds of years. Proper care will also help maintain the value of your instrument.

Production: Frank J. Hackinson
Production Coordinators: Philip Groeber and Rachel O'Kaine
Cover Design: Terpstra Design, San Francisco
Text Design and Layout: Susan Pinkerton

Illustrations: Michael Schmidt
Engraving: Tempo Music Press, Inc.
Printer: Tempo Music Press, Inc.

THE FJH MUSIC COMPANY INC.
Frank J. Hackinson

Visit us on the web at www.fjhmusic.com
ISBN 1-56939-577-4

To be a successful bassist, it is very important to learn proper BODY POSTURE.

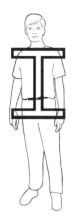

Here are the 5 important points for correct body posture:

1. Feet on floor in line with shoulders
2. Make an "I-Beam" with shoulders, spine, and hips
3. Shoulders in line with hips (do not twist)
4. Head in line with spine
5. Sit tall

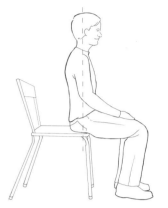

Remember: Correct posture is very important for good health and good playing!

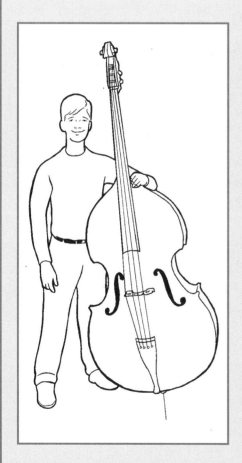

To correctly hold the double bass:

1. Stand or sit tall (make an "I-Beam")

2. Evenly distribute weight on BOTH legs and feet when you stand OR on your SEAT when you sit

3. Keep shoulders parallel to the floor with your trunk straight and tall

4. Bass should lean to you so that you are more beside than behind the instrument resting on your hip

5. Adjust the endpin so that you can reach the scroll with your left hand and the bridge with the middle knuckle of your middle finger of the right hand

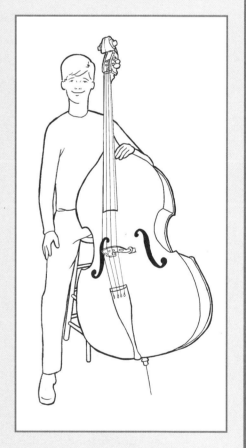

Icons used in *New Directions™ For Strings*

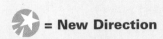 = **New Direction**   = **National Standard**   = **Pencil Game**   = **Review (checkpoint)**

STRING NAMES

E A D G

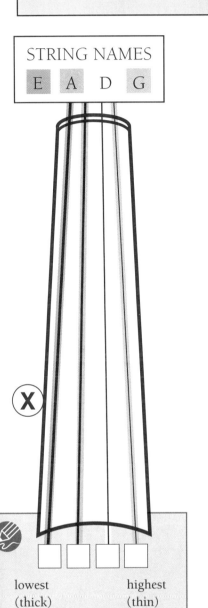

X

lowest
(thick)

highest
(thin)

Name your strings.

Plucking Your Strings

(1) TUNING TRACK

(**X**) = thumb spot

 Pizzicato (*pizz.*) = pluck the strings

(2) STRING CYCLE IN 4

G G G G | D D D D | A A A A | E E E E ‖

(3) STRING CYCLE IN 3

E E E | A A A | D D D | G G G ‖

 Improvise = to create music

 Making Music with D and A

Use these notes to improvise: D and A

Class Part:

D D D D | A A A A | D D D D | A A D D ‖

For each tune: **1. Clap and Count**   **2. Clap and Sing**   **3. *Pizzicato***

(4) MARCH IN 4

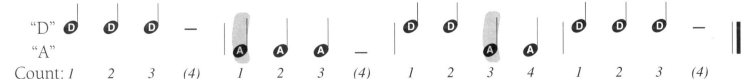

"D" D D D — | D D — | D D | D D D — ‖
"A"   A A A — | A A |
Count: 1 2 3 (4) 1 2 3 (4) 1 2 3 4 1 2 3 (4)

(5) WALTZ IN 3

"D" D D D | D — — | D D D | D — — | D — — ‖
"A"   A A A | A — — | A A A |
Count: 1 2 3 1 2 3 1 (2) (3) 1 2 3 1 2 3 1 (2) (3) 1 2 3 1 2 3 1 (2) (3)

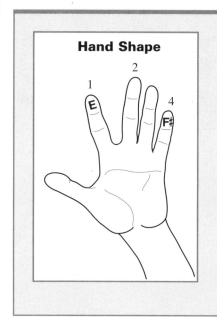

Hand Shape

On the Instrument

Fingers should contact fingerboard.

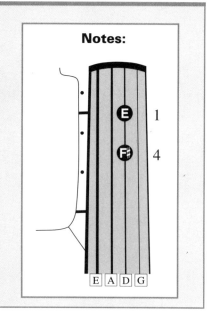

Notes:

For each tune: 1. Clap and Count   2. Clap and Sing   3. *Pizzicato*

6 FINGER PREPARATION ON F♯

F♯ F♯ F♯ - |F♯ F♯ F♯ - |
F♯ F♯ F♯ F♯ |F♯ F♯ F♯ - ‖

7 FINGER PREPARATION ON E

E E E |E - - |E E E |E - - |
E E E |E E E |E E E |E - - ‖

8 FINGER PREPARATION ON F♯, E, AND D

D E D E |D E F♯ F♯ |
E D E F♯ |D D D - ‖

9 HOT CROSS BUNS

F♯ E D - |F♯ E D - |
D D E E |F♯ E D - ‖

10 MARY HAD A LITTLE LAMB

F♯ E D E |F♯ F♯ F♯ - |
E E E - |F♯ F♯ F♯ - |
F♯ E D E |F♯ F♯ F♯ F♯ |
E E F♯ E |D - - - ‖

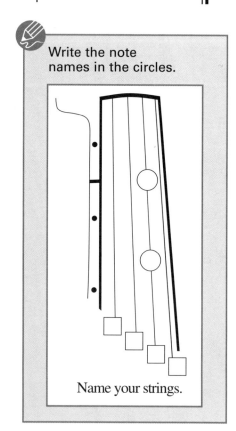

Write the note names in the circles.

Name your strings.

Continue to review these tunes as you learn the next pages.

SB303DB(A)

Reading/Writing music is a combination of a ladder  and a ruler.

You can:
• Step higher or lower on a ladder
• Measure length with a ruler

 Clef = **F** = establishes the lines and spaces for your instrument

The double bass uses the bass or F clef.

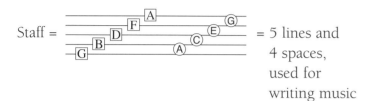 Staff = = 5 lines and 4 spaces, used for writing music

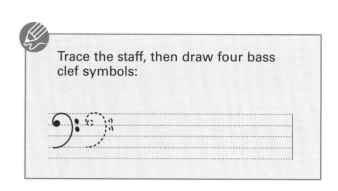

Trace the staff, then draw four bass clef symbols:

NOTE AND REST SYMBOLS

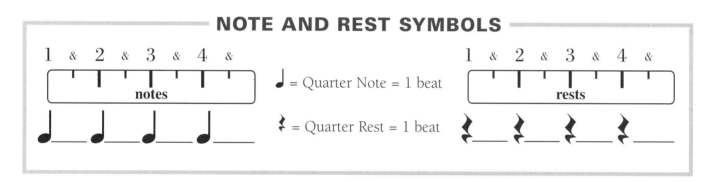

♩ = Quarter Note = 1 beat

𝄽 = Quarter Rest = 1 beat

This is A   This is D

For each tune: **1. Clap and Count**   **2. Clap and Sing**   **3.** *Pizzicato*

(11) MARCH ON A

(12) WALTZ ON D

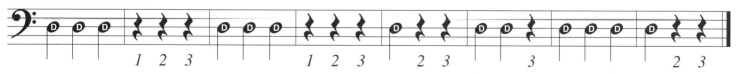

Write your own composition using quarter notes D and A, and quarter rests.

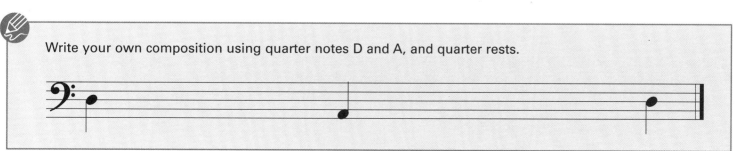

SB303DB(A)

MORE MUSIC SYMBOLS

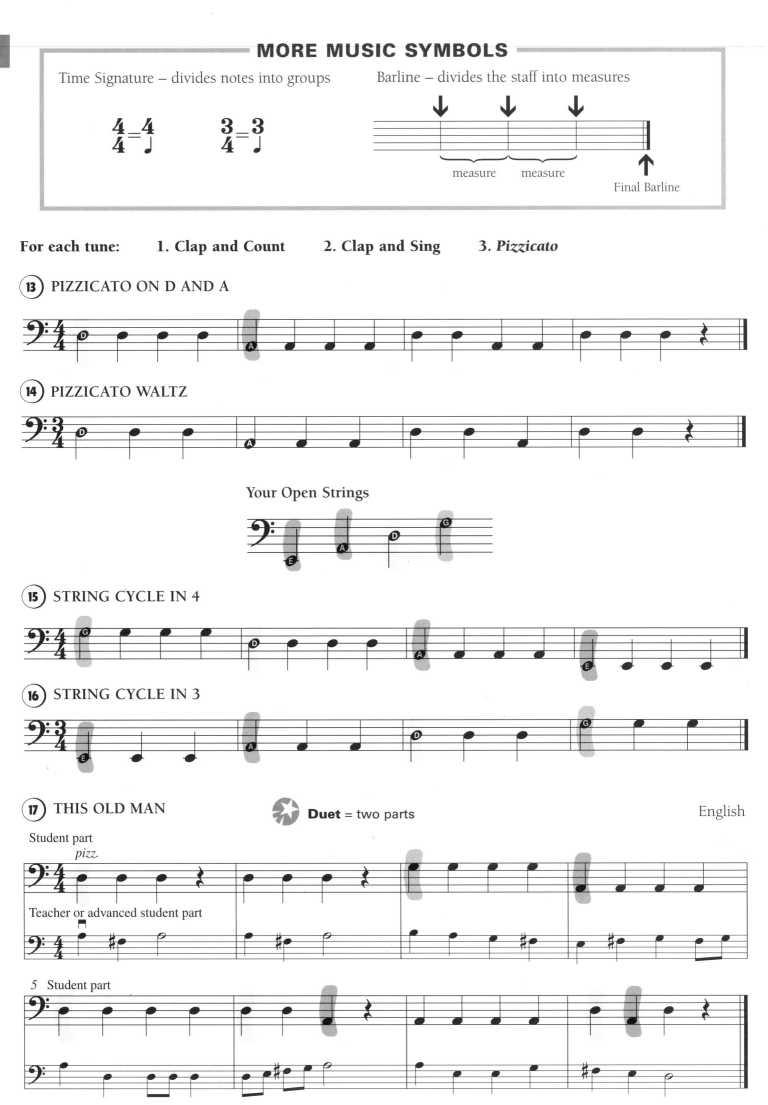

Time Signature – divides notes into groups

Barline – divides the staff into measures

measure   measure

Final Barline

For each tune: 1. Clap and Count   2. Clap and Sing   3. *Pizzicato*

13 PIZZICATO ON D AND A

14 PIZZICATO WALTZ

Your Open Strings

15 STRING CYCLE IN 4

16 STRING CYCLE IN 3

17 THIS OLD MAN

Duet = two parts

English

Student part
pizz.

Teacher or advanced student part

5 Student part

NOTE AND REST SYMBOLS

♩ = Half Note = 2 beats

▬ = Half Rest = 2 beats

Circle *Pizzicato* = circular motion of your right arm

This motion prepares the bow stroke.

Time Signature $\frac{4}{4} = 4$ ♩ $\frac{3}{4} = 3$ ♩

Cycles with Circles

18 BARCAROLLE

Jacques Offenbach

Student part

Teacher or advanced student part

5 Student part

19 AT PIERROT'S DOOR

French

Student part

Teacher or advanced student part

Complete the measures with ♩, ▬, ♩, 𝄽, using your open string notes or rests (4 beats per measure).

Name and then perform your piece. _____

= **Repeat Sign** = go back and play the line or section of music again

20 CHEERLEADING DUET

Duet

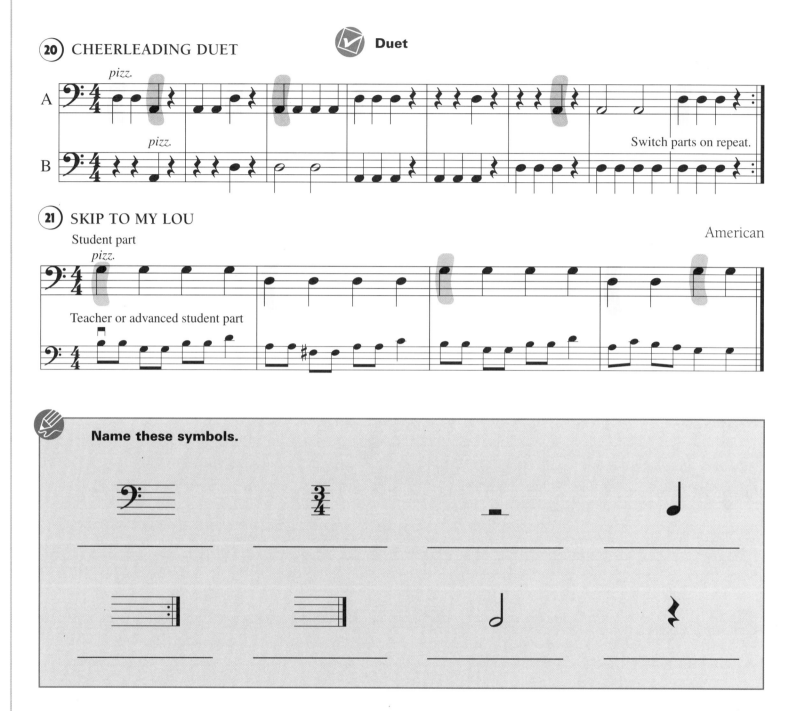

21 SKIP TO MY LOU

American

Name these symbols.

IMPROVISATION LOOP

Take your turn improvising while the class plays *pizz.*

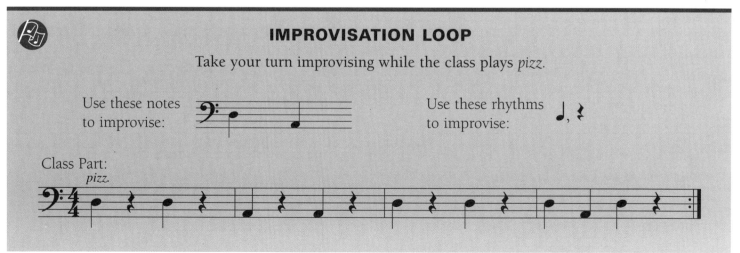

Use these notes to improvise:

Use these rhythms to improvise:

Class Part:
pizz.

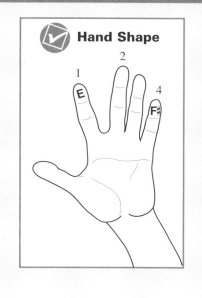

Hand Shape

On the Instrument

Fingers should contact fingerboard.

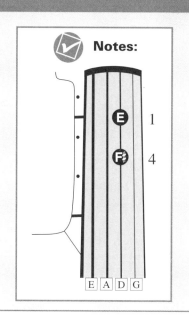

Notes:

MUSIC ALPHABET AND LEDGER LINES

Music Alphabet = the letter names of music notes: A, B, C, D, E, F, G
Once you reach **G,** you begin again with **A**.

Learning F#, E, and D

Ledger Lines = lines that extend the staff above and below

For each tune: **1. Clap and Count**   **2. Clap and Sing**   **3. *Pizzicato***

22 PRACTICING F#

23 PRACTICING E

24 FINGER MIX UP

25 HOT CROSS BUNS

English

26 MARY HAD A LITTLE LAMB—Memorize this piece.

Sarah J. Hale

 Contact Points for the Left Hand:

1. Thumb under the neck, aligned with 2nd finger

2. Hand is in a curved "C" shape

3. Base knuckles are parallel to the neck with the pads of the fingertips contacting the strings (keep forearm aligned from elbow to wrist)

4th finger strum

 + = Left-Hand *Pizzicato* (using 4th finger)

27 D-A-D SONG

28 UP ON THE HOUSETOP

Benjamin R. Hanby

NOTE AND REST SYMBOLS

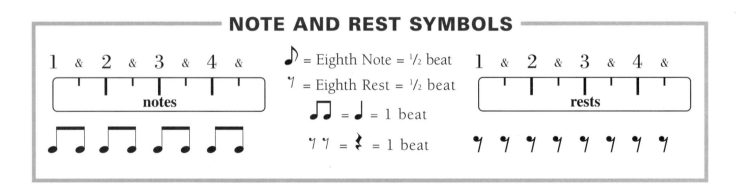

29 PERPETUAL EIGHTH NOTES

30 BARN DANCE

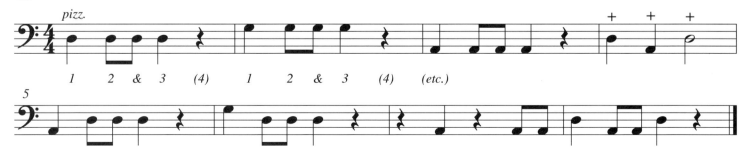

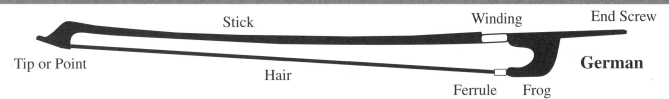

Stick   Winding   End Screw

Tip or Point   Hair   Ferrule   Frog   **German**

 Bow Hold Steps

GERMAN

FRENCH

1. Base hand knuckles parallel to frog
2. Thumb and index finger make a circle around the bow stick, thumb on top
3. Middle and ring fingers in the cut-out of frog
4. Pinky fingertip is placed under the frog on the ferrule
5. Check for a space between the frog and your palm

1. Base knuckles parallel to stick with wrist slightly lower than the knuckles
2. Bent thumb is placed in the cut-out of the frog
3. Check that the middle fingertip is on the ferrule
4. Ring and pinky fingers gently curve over the bow stick
5. Lean slightly on the index finger

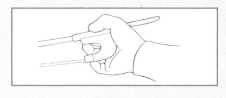

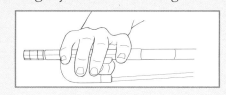

 Arco = to play using the bow. (*Arco* is the Italian word for bow). We always play *arco* unless directions say *pizz.*

⋁ = **Up bow** = moving bow toward frog   ☐ = **Down bow** = moving bow toward tip

Stick   Winding   End Screw

Tip or Point   Hair   Ferrule   Frog   **French**

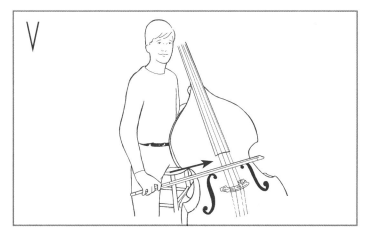

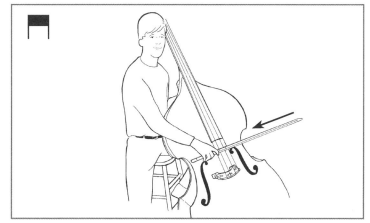

For these Bow Studies: 1. Air bow   2. Play on each string

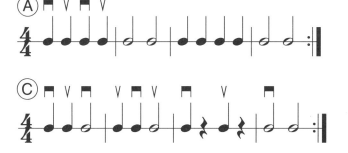

SB303DB(A)

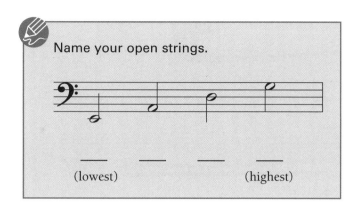

Name your open strings.

___ ___ ___ ___
(lowest)   (highest)

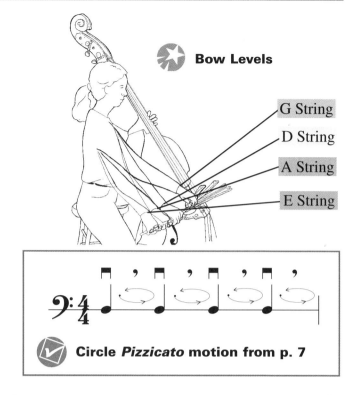

Bow Levels

G String
D String
A String
E String

❜ = **Bow Retake** = to lift the bow from the string and return to the frog in a circular motion

Circle *Pizzicato* motion from p. 7

For these Bow Studies: 1. Air bow and say bow direction 2. Play on your instrument 3. Memorize one Bow Study

31 TWO AT A TIME—Play two times: first time violas and cellos, second time violins and basses.

32 BOWING ON D

33 BOWING ON G

34 BOWING ON A

35 ARCO ACROBATICS

Write your own 4 measure *Arco Acrobatics* on D and A. Use quarter notes and half notes.

Dynamics describes the level of sound, (softer or louder).

p = *piano* = play softly, or *f* = *forte* = play loudly, with a full tone

With the bow, play your E, A, D, and G strings at a *piano* then ***forte*** dynamic.

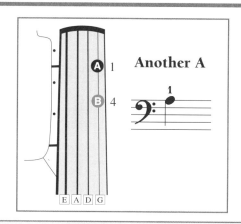

Another A

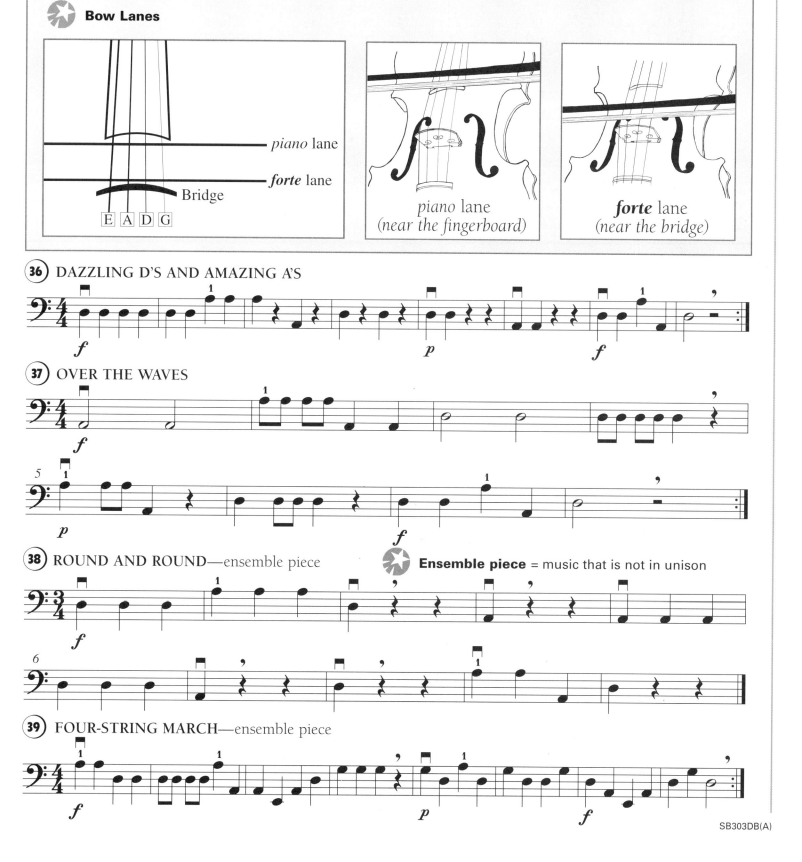

Bow Lanes

piano lane
forte lane
Bridge
E A D G

piano lane
(near the fingerboard)

forte lane
(near the bridge)

36 DAZZLING D'S AND AMAZING A'S

f   *p*   *f*

37 OVER THE WAVES

f

5

p   *f*

38 ROUND AND ROUND—ensemble piece

Ensemble piece = music that is not in unison

f

6

39 FOUR-STRING MARCH—ensemble piece

f   *p*   *f*

SB303DB(A)

Tetrachord = a 4-note pattern

Tetrachords can go
UP (like D, E, F♯, G) or
DOWN (like G, F♯, E, D).

Note Names:	G	F♯	E	D
Finger Numbers:	0	4	1	0
Solfège Syllables:	FA -	MI -	RE -	DO

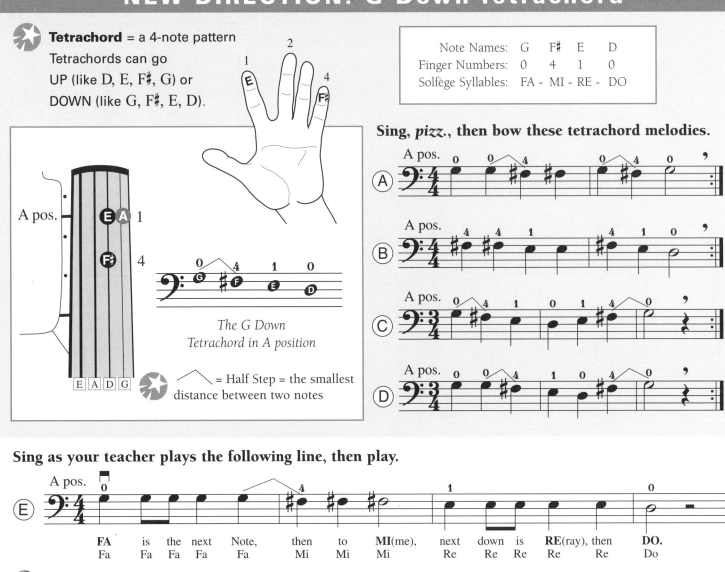

A pos.

The G Down
Tetrachord in A position

⌐ = Half Step = the smallest distance between two notes

Sing, *pizz.*, then bow these tetrachord melodies.

(A) A pos.

(B) A pos.

(C) A pos.

(D) A pos.

Sing as your teacher plays the following line, then play.

(E) A pos.

| **FA** | is | the | next | Note, | then | to | **MI**(me), | next | down | is | **RE**(ray), then | **DO.** |
| Fa | Fa | Fa | Fa | Fa | | Mi | Mi | Mi | Re | Re | Re | Re | Re | Do |

40 OH, GEE DOWN

A pos.

f

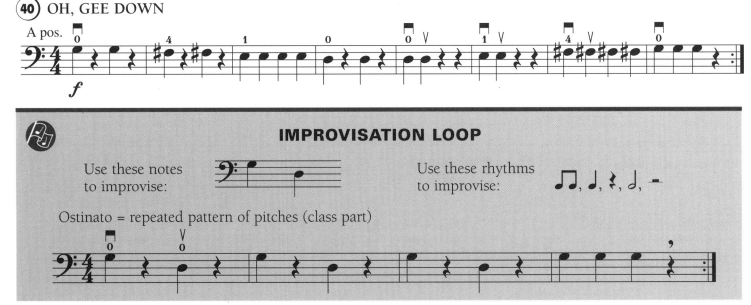

IMPROVISATION LOOP

Use these notes
to improvise:

Use these rhythms
to improvise:

Ostinato = repeated pattern of pitches (class part)

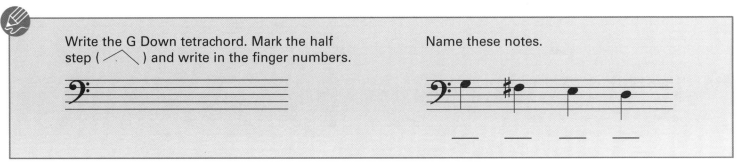

Write the G Down tetrachord. Mark the half
step (⌐) and write in the finger numbers.

Name these notes.

____ ____ ____ ____

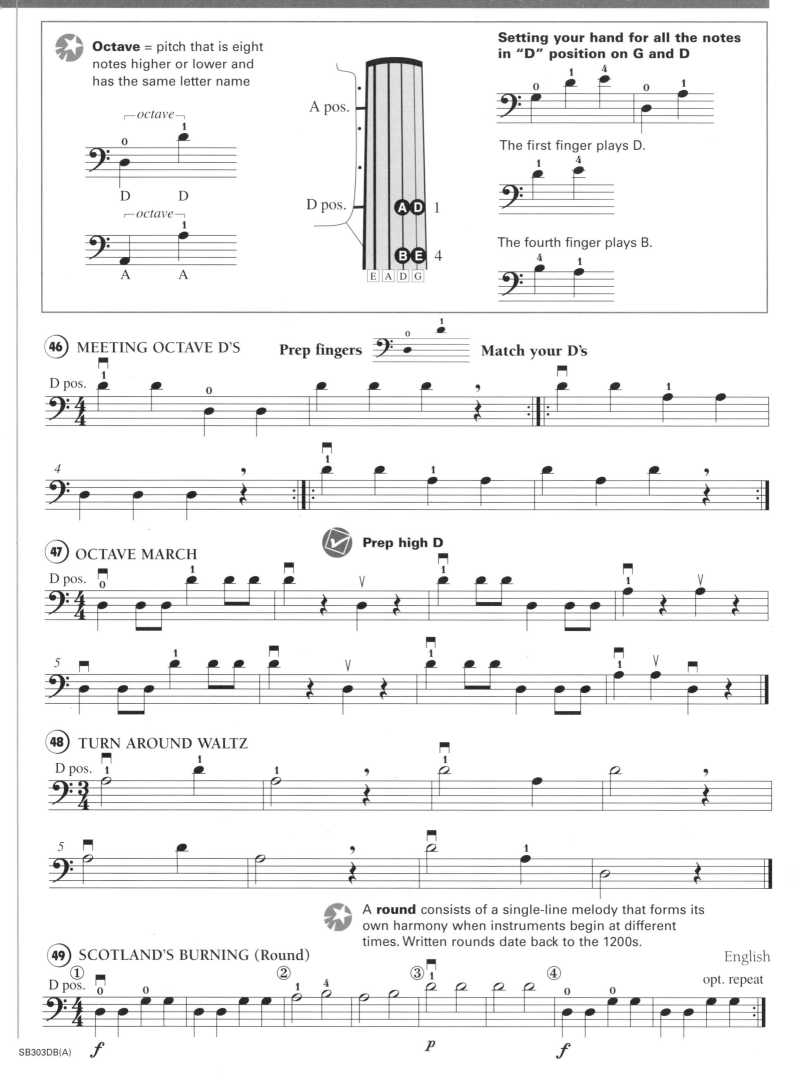

Pizzicato each tune before bowing!

⭐ — = **Shift** = move hand to a new position

55 SONG OF THE WIND — German

56 BADGE MARCH—ensemble piece

57 CAMPTOWN RACES—ensemble piece — Stephen Foster

58 BAA BAA BLACK SHEEP—ensemble piece — English

Spell the words by naming the notes.

With Octave D's in Tune, We Now Add C♯

⭐ **The D Down Tetrachord** = D - C♯ - B - A

Note Names:	D	C♯	B	A
Finger Numbers:	2	1	pvt.4	1
Solfège Syllables:	DO -	TI -	LA -	SO

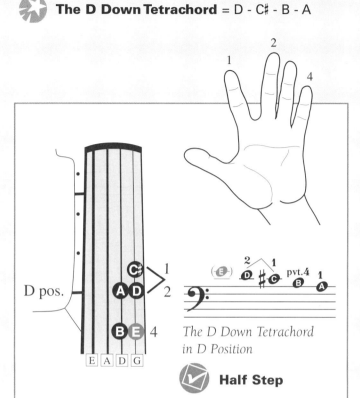

The D Down Tetrachord in D Position

✓ **Half Step**

Sing, *pizz.*, then bow these tetrachord melodies.

Sing as your teacher plays the following line, then play.

DO is the Bot-tom Note, **DO** is the High-er Note, now we sing **DOWN** the scale.
Do Do Do Do Do Do   Do Do Do Do Do Do   Do Do Do Ti La So

IMPROVISATION LOOP

Use these notes to improvise:

Use these rhythms to improvise:

Ostinato Part:

59 SNOWSHOE DANCE   ✓ **Prep fingers**

60 SPRINGTIME STOMP   ✕ = foot stomp

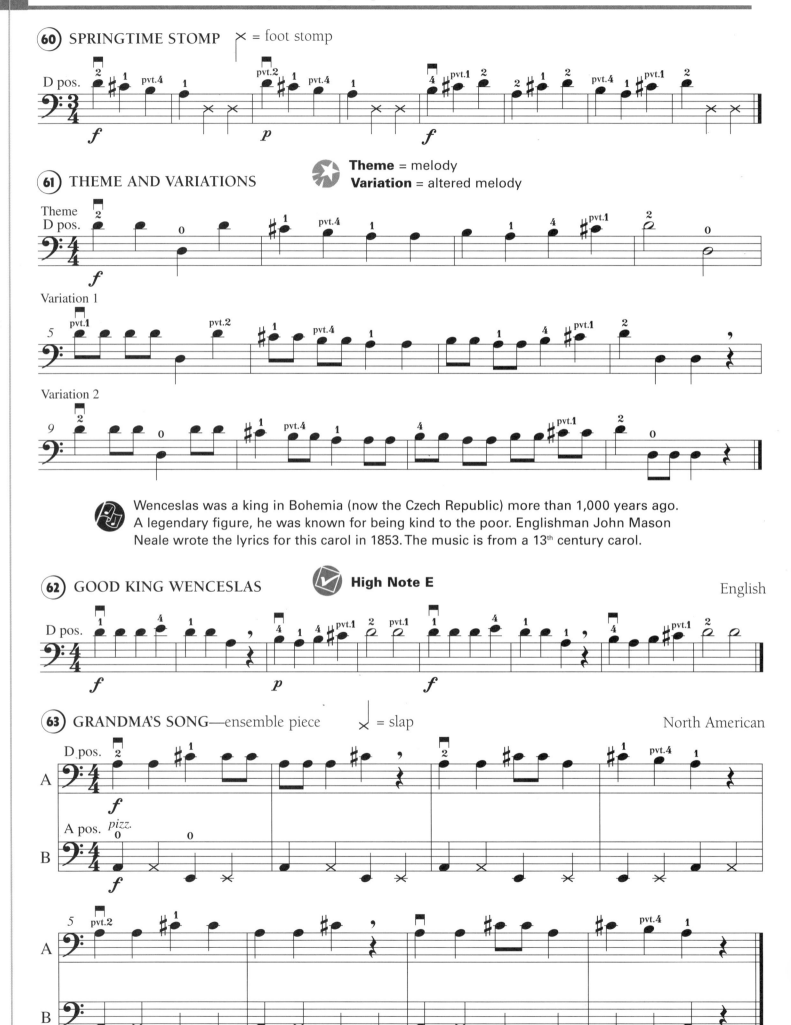

61 THEME AND VARIATIONS

Theme = melody
Variation = altered melody

> Wenceslas was a king in Bohemia (now the Czech Republic) more than 1,000 years ago. A legendary figure, he was known for being kind to the poor. Englishman John Mason Neale wrote the lyrics for this carol in 1853. The music is from a 13th century carol.

62 GOOD KING WENCESLAS   **High Note E**   English

63 GRANDMA'S SONG—ensemble piece   ✕ = slap   North American

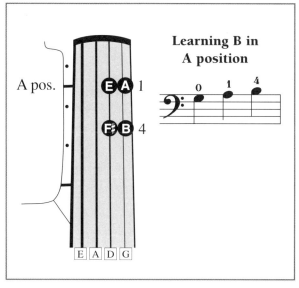

Learning B in A position

Fourth Finger Study Starting on D

Ode to Joy is from Beethoven's *Symphony No. 9.* When it was first performed in 1824, Beethoven was completely deaf. He did not notice the audience's applause at the end of the symphony until it was pointed out to him.

64 ODE TO JOY

Ludwig van Beethoven

65 SPIDER WALK—*ensemble piece*

66 ARE YOU SLEEPING? (**Round**)—Memorize this piece.

French

67 CHICKEN ON A FENCE POST—*ensemble piece*   ✗ = slap

North American

SB303DB(A)

EXTENDING THE BOW STROKE

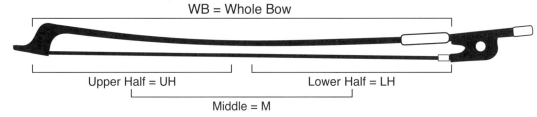

WB = Whole Bow
Upper Half = UH
Lower Half = LH
Middle = M

NOTE AND REST SYMBOLS

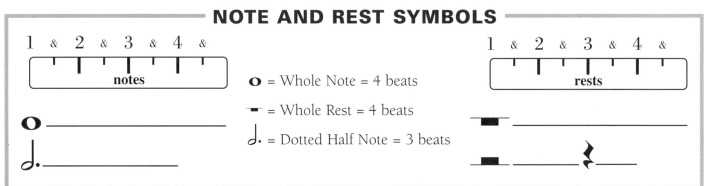

o = Whole Note = 4 beats

▬ = Whole Rest = 4 beats

♩. = Dotted Half Note = 3 beats

Bow Studies—Play on each string. Keep your bow moving!

68 BOW STUDY ONE

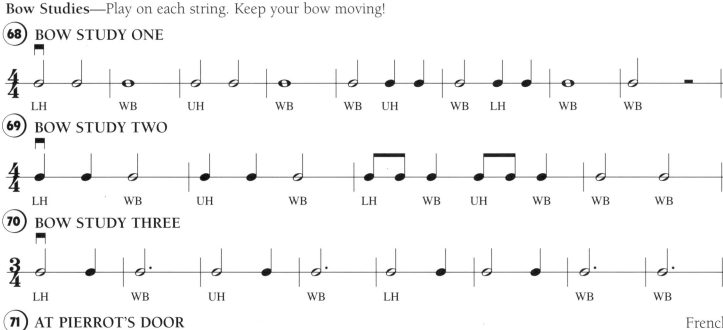

69 BOW STUDY TWO

70 BOW STUDY THREE

71 AT PIERROT'S DOOR   French

A pos.

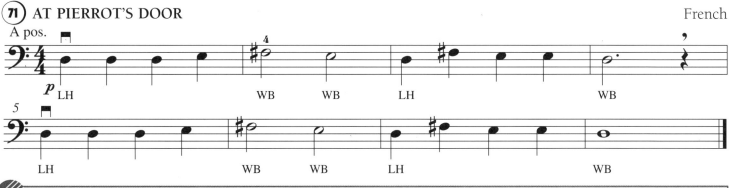

p

5

Balancing Act - Write one note on the right side to equal the note values on the left.

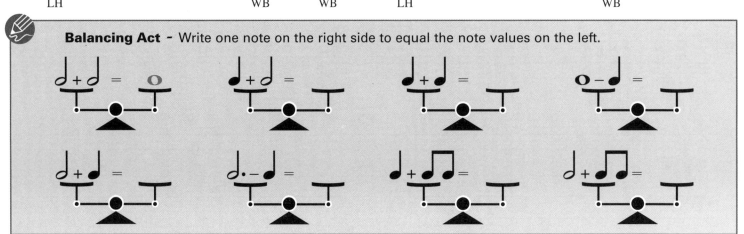

72 GO TELL AUNT RHODY

Bow Lanes

American

73 HOME FROM SCHOOL (*Hui jia qü*)

Chinese

Antonio Vivaldi (1678–1741), an Italian violinist, was known as the "red priest" because of his red hair. Vivaldi was in charge of music at an orphanage for girls in Venice. He wrote over 500 concerti. The piece below is from the concerto, *The Four Seasons.*

74 SPRING

Antonio Vivaldi

Name the tetrachords.

Scale = tetrachord + tetrachord
Scales begin and end on the same letter name.

 Key Signature identifies notes
that are raised or lowered.

 Whole step = two half steps

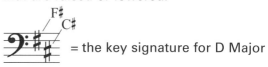 = the key signature for D Major

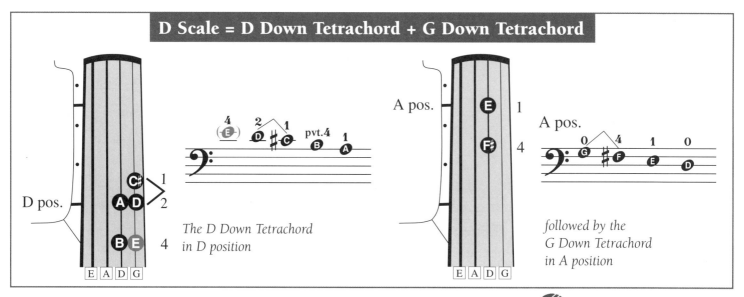

D Scale = D Down Tetrachord + G Down Tetrachord

The D Down Tetrachord in D position

followed by the G Down Tetrachord in A position

1. Clap and Sing   2. *Pizz.*   3. *Arco*

Note Names:	D	C#	B	A	G	F#	E	D
Finger Numbers:	2	1	pvt.4	1	0	−4	1	0
Solfège Syllables:	Do	Ti	La	La	So	So	Fa	Fa	Mi	Mi	Re	Do

Sing and play up the scale.

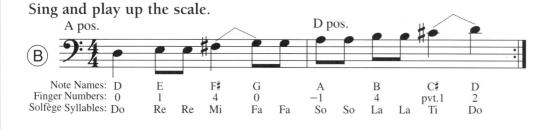

Note Names:	D	E	F#	G	A	B	C#	D
Finger Numbers:	0	1	4	0	−1	4	pvt.1	2
Solfège Syllables:	Do	Re	Re	Mi	Fa	Fa	So	So	La	La	Ti	Do

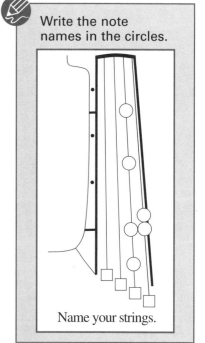

Write the note names in the circles.

Name your strings.

SCALE STUDIES

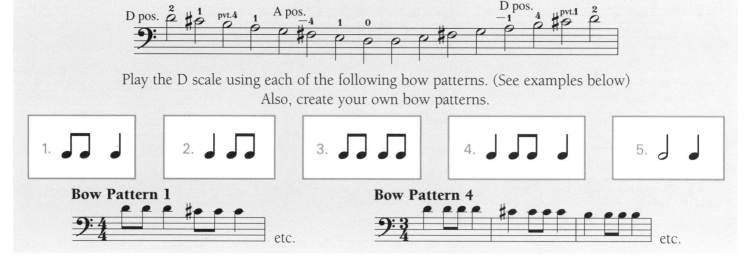

Play the D scale using each of the following bow patterns. (See examples below)
Also, create your own bow patterns.

1.   2.   3.   4.   5.

Bow Pattern 1

etc.

Bow Pattern 4

etc.

75 FRENCH FOLK SONG

French

◉ 𝅗𝅥. = **Dotted Half Note** = 3 beats

76 OH! HOW LOVELY IS THE EVENING (Round)

English

🎼 Jacques Offenbach (1819–1880) was a composer of popular music for the theater in France. He played violin and was a virtuoso cellist. "Can Can" was written in 1858 for his operetta, *Orpheus in the Underworld*.

77 CAN CAN—Memorize this piece.

Jacques Offenbach

SB303DB(A)

New Bowing Styles

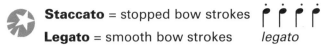

Staccato = stopped bow strokes
Legato = smooth bow strokes *legato*

78 JUMPING JACKS—Half class *pizz.*, half class match with staccato stroke.

79 POP! GOES THE WEASEL

English

80 GROUND ROUND

Melody = main tune
Harmony = pitches that accompany the melody

81 TWINKLE, MY EYE—ensemble piece

German

♩. = **Dotted Quarter Note** = 1½ beats

1 and ½ beats = ♩ + ♪ or ♪ + ♪ + ♪

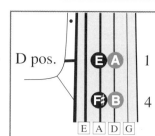

D pos.

A new position for E and F♯ on the A string in D position—Refer to the bass fingerboard graphic at the end of the book

82 DOTTED QUARTER STUDY: **1. Clap and Count**   **2. Clap and Sing**   **3. Play**

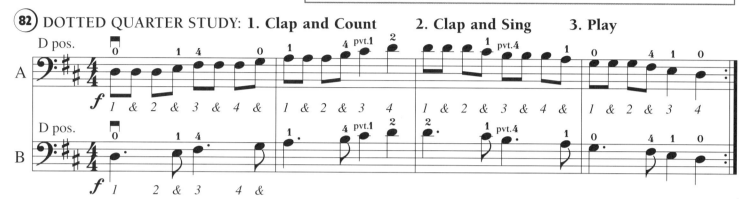

Antonín Dvořák (1841–1904) was from Bohemia, which is now the Czech Republic. He played violin in church and in village bands. He was influenced by spirituals and African-American folk songs while he lived in America from 1892–1895. His Ninth Symphony, "From the New World," included *Goin' Home,* a slave song.

83 GOIN' HOME

Antonín Dvořák

84 LONDON BRIDGE

English

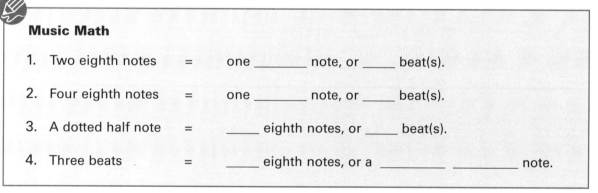

Music Math

1. Two eighth notes   =   one _____ note, or _____ beat(s).

2. Four eighth notes   =   one _____ note, or _____ beat(s).

3. A dotted half note   =   _____ eighth notes, or _____ beat(s).

4. Three beats   .   =   _____ eighth notes, or a _____ _____ note.

85 MAY SONG   **E and F♯ in D position**   German

BOW DIVISION = part of bow used (UH, LH, WB)

Name the Parts and Bow Divisions.

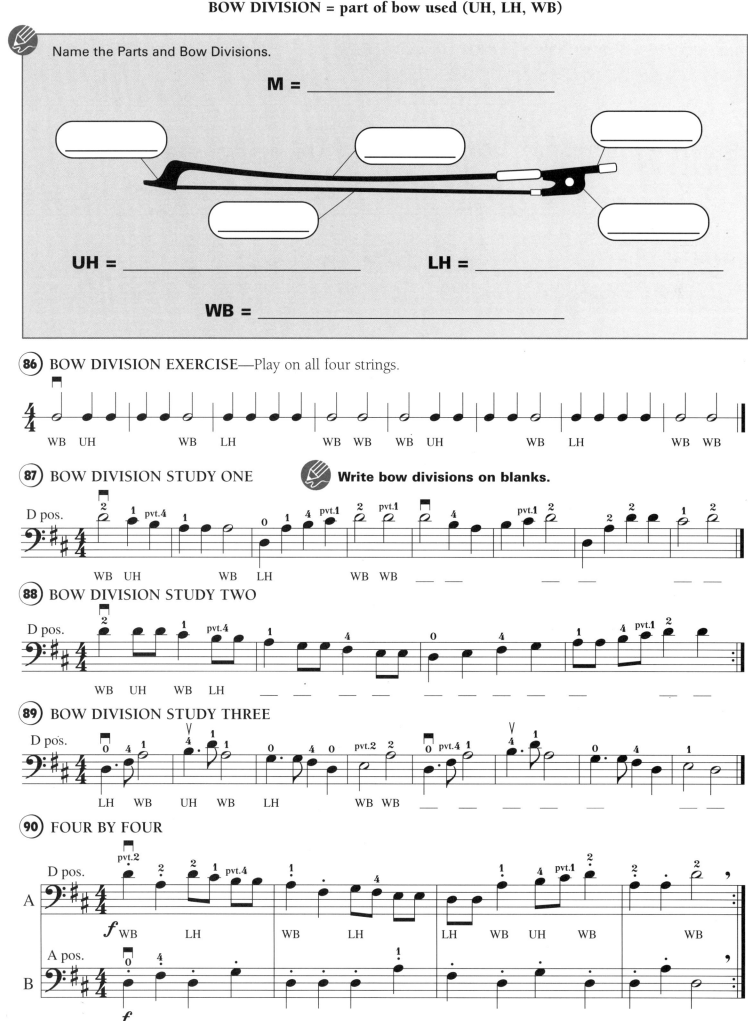

M = _____

UH = _____

LH = _____

WB = _____

86 **BOW DIVISION EXERCISE**—Play on all four strings.

WB   UH   WB   LH   WB   WB   WB   UH   WB   LH   WB   WB

87 BOW DIVISION STUDY ONE   **Write bow divisions on blanks.**

D pos.

WB   UH   WB   LH   WB   WB   __   __   __   __   __

88 BOW DIVISION STUDY TWO

D pos.

WB   UH   WB   LH   __   __

89 BOW DIVISION STUDY THREE

D pos.

LH   WB   UH   WB   LH   WB   WB   __   __   __   __   __

90 FOUR BY FOUR

D pos.

A

f WB   LH   WB   LH   LH   WB   UH   WB   WB

A pos.

B

f

91 STYLES À LA MUSIQUE

Staccato and Finger Tunnels

Upbeat = note(s) that appears before the first barline. The upbeat is subtracted from the last measure of music.

92 SARASPONDA

Dutch

Using Key Signatures

Draw four F#s like the one below.

Draw four C#s like the one below.

If a sharp is written at the beginning of a piece, you play all those same pitches as sharps. This is called the **key signature**. Draw your clef and the D major key signature below.

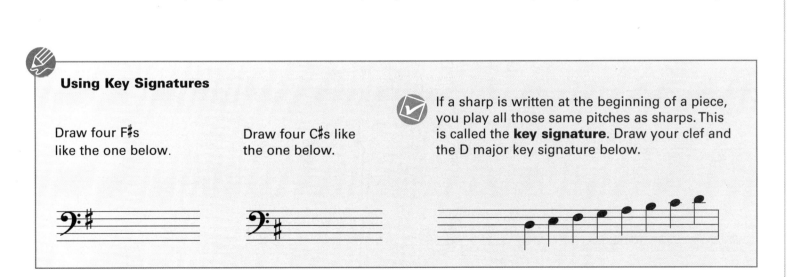

ADVANCED MUSICIANSHIP

Good Sound, Big Tone = the correct combination of bow speed, arm weight, and contact point (bow lane)

Crescendo = Play Louder = more bow speed or more weight, with bow nearer the bridge:

Diminuendo = Play Softer = less bow speed or less weight, with bow nearer the fingerboard:

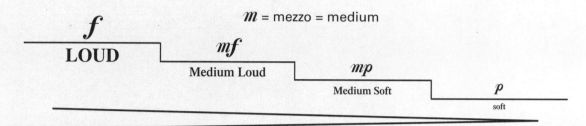

m = mezzo = medium

f LOUD

mf Medium Loud

mp Medium Soft

p soft

93 MELODY MYSTERY: **1. Clap and Sing**   **2. Play**   **3. Guess the Tune**

94 COUNTRY GARDENS   *f–p* = *f* first time, *p* on the repeat   English

f–p = *f* first time, *p* on the repeat

William Billings (1746–1800) was a self-taught composer. He was a friend of revolutionary leaders Paul Revere and Samuel Adams. *Chester* was the unofficial anthem of the American Revolution, along with *Yankee Doodle*.

95 CHESTER   William Billings

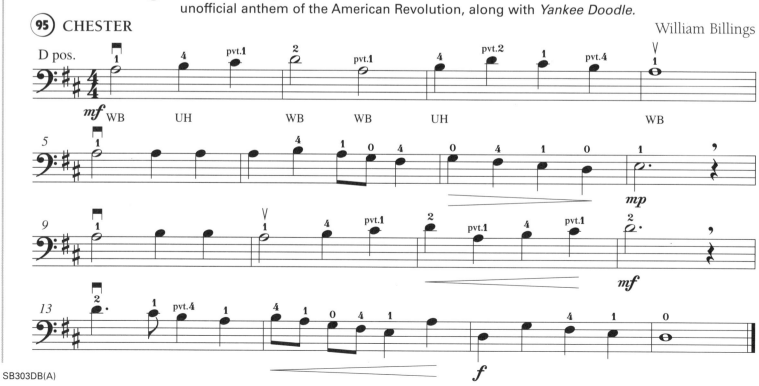

Stephen Foster (1826–1864) was an American songwriter. *Oh! Susanna* was the "marching song" for the California Gold Rush of 1849 and was the unofficial theme song for wagon trains going west.

96) OH! SUSANNA — **Upbeat** — Stephen Foster

Johannes Brahms (1833–1897), a German composer, studied cello, piano, and French horn in his youth. He composed large works such as symphonies, as well as chamber music, piano pieces, songs, and choral music. Brahms, J.S. Bach, and Beethoven are known as the "Three B's" of music.

97) LULLABY — Johannes Brahms

98) FIRST CONCERT PIECE—ensemble piece — Elliot Del Borgo

Maestoso

⭐ **The C Down Tetrachord** = C - B - A - G

Note Names:	C	B	A	G
Finger Numbers:	2	1	0	2
Solfège Syllables:	FA -	MI -	RE -	DO

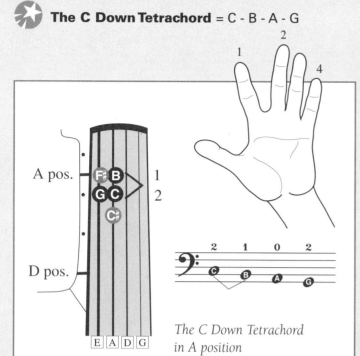

The C Down Tetrachord in A position

Sing, *pizz.*, then bow these tetrachord melodies.

1. Clap and Sing   2. *Pizz.*   3. *Arco*

Ⓔ

C Down Town

Waltzin' in C

IMPROVISATION LOOP

Use these notes to improvise:

Use these rhythms to improvise:

Class Part:

101 HIKING IN THE CANYON

102 COPY CAT—ensemble piece

103 GOOD KING WENCESLAS II

English

104 THE ELEPHANT—Memorize this piece.

Folk Song

105 GRANDMA'S SONG II—ensemble piece

✗ = slap

North American

106 THE TRAIN

rit. = *Ritardando* = slowing down

Folk Song

NEW DIRECTION: G Major Scale

 = the key signature for G Major

G Scale = G Down Tetrachord + C Down Tetrachord

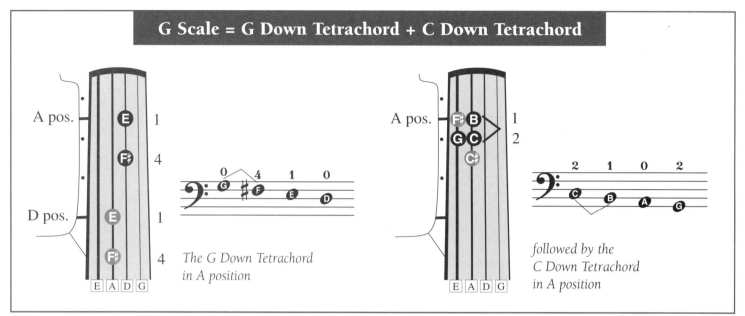

The G Down Tetrachord in A position

followed by the C Down Tetrachord in A position

1. Clap and Sing   2. *Pizz*.   3. *Arco*

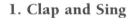

Note Names:	G	F♯	E	D	C	B	A	G
Finger Numbers:	0	4	1	0	2	1	0	2
Solfège Syllables:	Do Do	Ti	La La	So	Fa	Mi Mi	Re Re	Do

Note Names:	G	A	B	C	D	E	F♯	G
Finger Numbers:	2	0	1	2	0	1	4	0
Solfège Syllables:	Do	Re Re	Mi Mi	Fa	So So	La La	Ti	Do

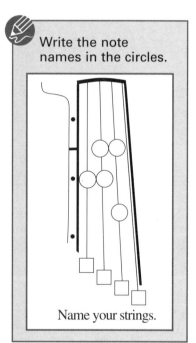

Write the note names in the circles.

Name your strings.

SCALE STUDIES

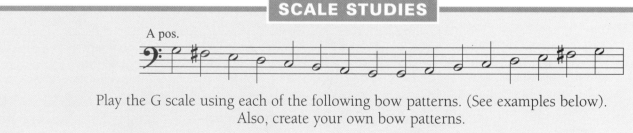

Play the G scale using each of the following bow patterns. (See examples below).
Also, create your own bow patterns.

 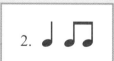   

Bow Pattern 1

 etc.

Bow Pattern 4

 etc.

107 LA CLOCHE (Round)   French

108 OLD MACDONALD   North American

109 SWEET BETSY FROM PIKE   North American

☑ — = shift

110 FROGGIE GOES A' COURTIN'   North American

Switch parts on repeat.

Name the tetrachords, then write the tetrachords and the G Major scale.

_____   _____   _____   _____

G Down tetrachord   C Down tetrachord   G Major scale

111 SLUR PREPARATION ～＝ tap 1st finger freely

⭐ ⌣ = **Slur** = connecting different pitches in the same bow direction

112 G DOWN TETRACHORD SLURS

113 C DOWN TETRACHORD SLURS

114 SLUR MEETS THE G MAJOR SCALE

115 STARTING ON D

116 STARTING ON G

117 BUTTERSCOTCH WALTZ

String Crossing = moving the bow from one string to another

STOPPED Slurs—Stop the bow after each note.

SMOOTH Slurs—Keep the bow moving!

118 STOPPED SLURS UP-DOWN

119 SMOOTH CROSSINGS UP-DOWN

120 ODE TO JOY **(with slurs)**—Memorize this piece and watch your bow!   Ludwig van Beethoven

121 STOPPED SLURS COMBINATION

122 SMOOTH CROSSINGS COMBINATION

123 WAVY SLURS

More Bowing Styles

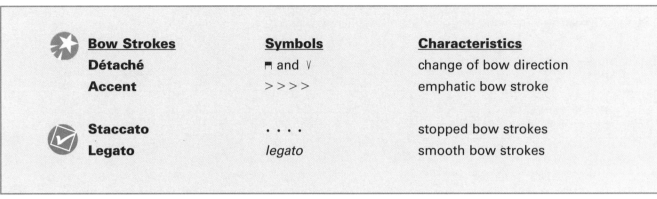

Bow Strokes	Symbols	Characteristics
Détaché	⊓ and V	change of bow direction
Accent	> > > >	emphatic bow stroke
Staccato	. . . .	stopped bow strokes
Legato	*legato*	smooth bow strokes

124 BOW STYLE STUDY—Play on each string.

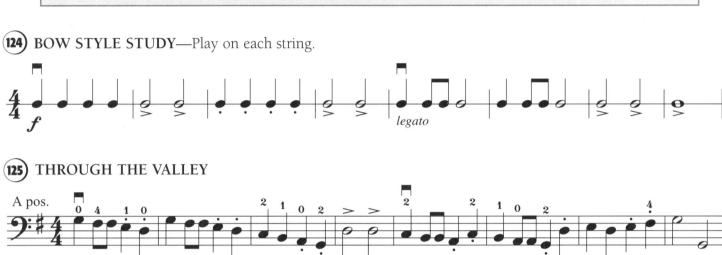

125 THROUGH THE VALLEY

126 TWISTING

— = shift

Write the bow stroke names on the blank spaces.

127 JIM ALONG JOSIE

North American

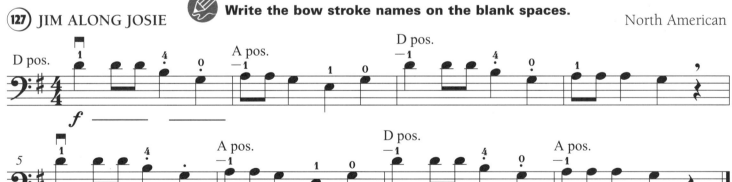

128 AURA LEE

Traditional

129 **PIECE PETITE**—ensemble piece

Elliot Del Borgo

String Crossing Study—Play on D and A.

130 **LONG, LONG AGO**

Traditional

Switch parts on repeat.

— = **Tie** = marking that connects notes of the same pitch together without a break

Bow Ties—Pay special attention to bow speed. Play on the D string.

 Jean Sibelius (1865–1957) composed music that described the people and country of his native Finland. *Finlandia* is identified with Finland's movement for independence and national identity.

(131) FINLANDIA—ensemble piece

Jean Sibelius

(132) SHALOM CHAVERIM

Hebrew

Upbeat

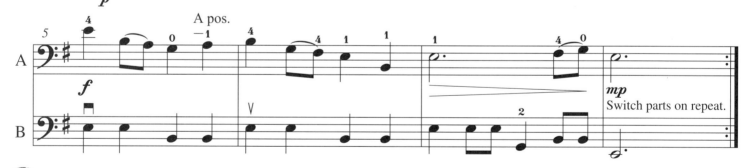

Circle the rhythm examples that are correct.

a.   b.   c.   d.   e.   f.   g.   h.   i.

Chromatic = moving up or down by half steps

 SHARP
The sharp (♯) raises a note by ½ step.

 NATURAL
The natural (♮) cancels a sharp or flat.

 FLAT
The flat (♭) lowers a note by ½ step.

 Accidentals = sharp, natural, and flat symbols for altering pitch

Draw three of each accidental.

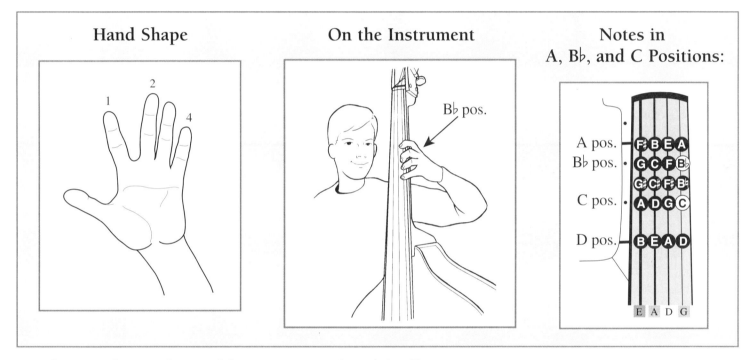

Hand Shape

On the Instrument

Notes in A, B♭, and C Positions:

For these Studies: violins and basses on E, violas and cellos on C

Accidental Study One

A pos.

Accidental Study Two

A pos.

(133) STRINGS HIGH AND LOW!

SB303DB(A)

Accidentals on All Strings

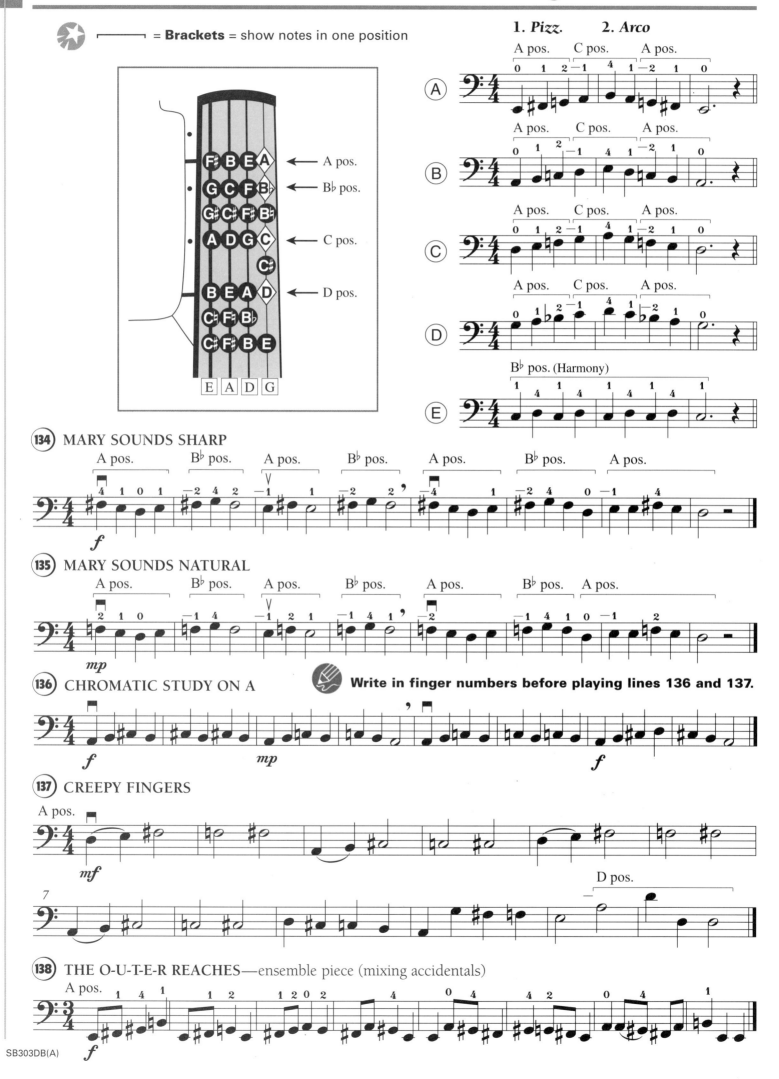

139) HOPSCOTCH!

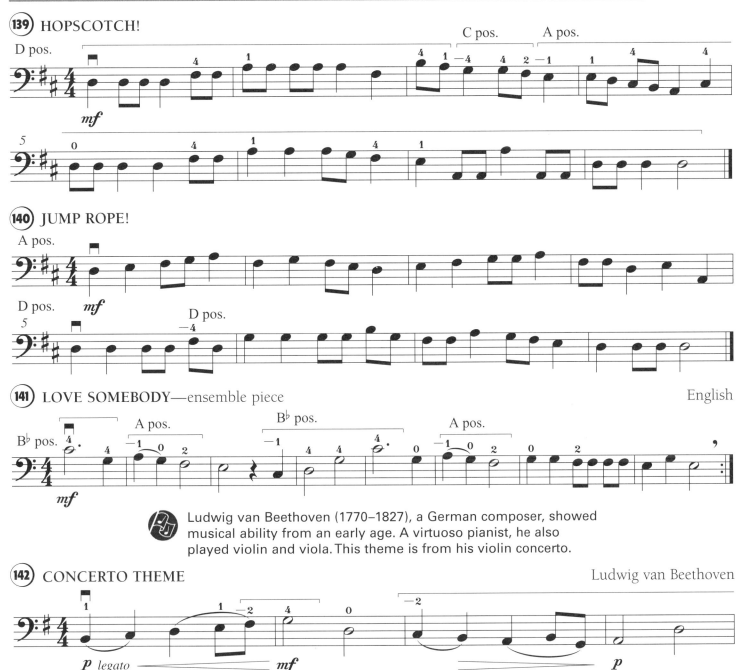

140) JUMP ROPE!

141) LOVE SOMEBODY—ensemble piece

English

Ludwig van Beethoven (1770–1827), a German composer, showed musical ability from an early age. A virtuoso pianist, he also played violin and viola. This theme is from his violin concerto.

142) CONCERTO THEME

Ludwig van Beethoven

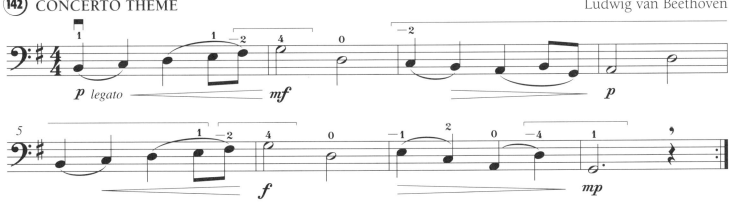

Kum Ba Yah (Come By Here) is from Gullah, an English-African creole language. The Gullah are people of African ancestry living on the Sea Islands of Georgia and South Carolina.

143) KUM BA YAH—ensemble piece

African American

144 CHROMATIC BOOGIE — Chromatic

145 BLUES ON ROUTE 259—Clap the A part rhythm pattern.

146 ACCIDENTAL BLUES—Find the A part repeated rhythms.

Yankee Doodle was written in the 1750s during the French and Indian War by British doctor Richard Shuckburg. Although the lyrics mocked the colonial Americans, they adopted the tune as their own.

(147) YANKEE DOODLE—ensemble piece (Memorize this piece.) English

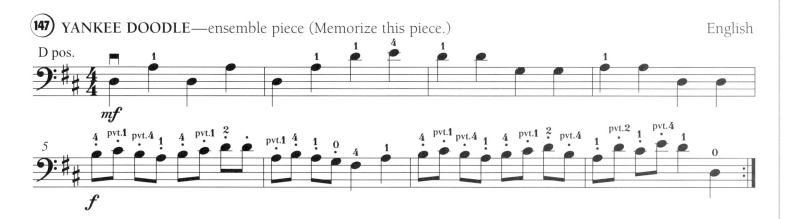

 The kookaburra is an Australian bird, the world's largest kingfisher. The kookaburra's song (cry) sounds like a human laughing.

(148) KOOKABURRA (Round) Australian

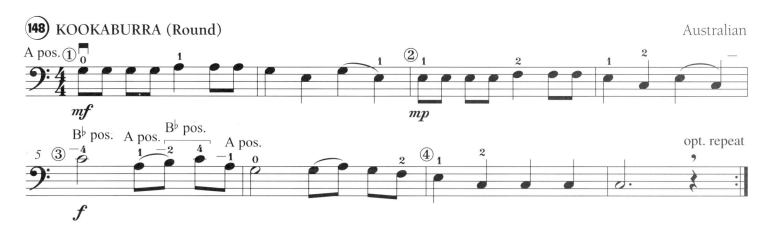

My Country 'Tis of Thee is known in England as *God Save the King/Queen.* The earliest printed version of this tune dates to 1744; the earliest known performance was in 1745. In the United States, *My Country 'Tis of Thee* shared status as the national anthem with the *Star-Spangled Banner* until 1931, when the *Star-Spangled Banner* became the official national anthem.

(149) AMERICA (My Country 'Tis of Thee) Lyrics: Samuel F. Smith
Music from Thesaurus Musicus

SB303DB(A)

NEW DIRECTION: C Major Scale

 The upper C Down Tetrachord and the F Down Tetrachord

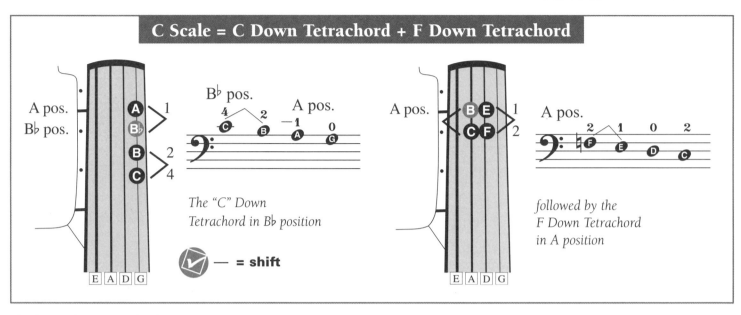

C Scale = C Down Tetrachord + F Down Tetrachord

The "C" Down Tetrachord in B♭ position

✓ — = shift

followed by the F Down Tetrachord in A position

1. Sing 2. Pizz. 3. Arco

SCALE STUDIES

Play the C scale using each of the following bow patterns. (See examples below).
Also, create your own bow patterns.

1. 2. 3. 4. 5.

Bow Pattern 1 etc.

Bow Pattern 2 etc.

Bow Pattern 4 etc.

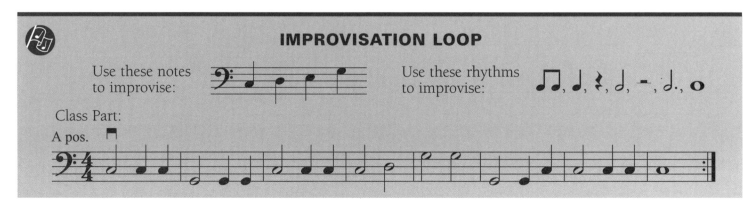

IMPROVISATION LOOP

Use these notes to improvise:

Use these rhythms to improvise:

Class Part:
A pos.

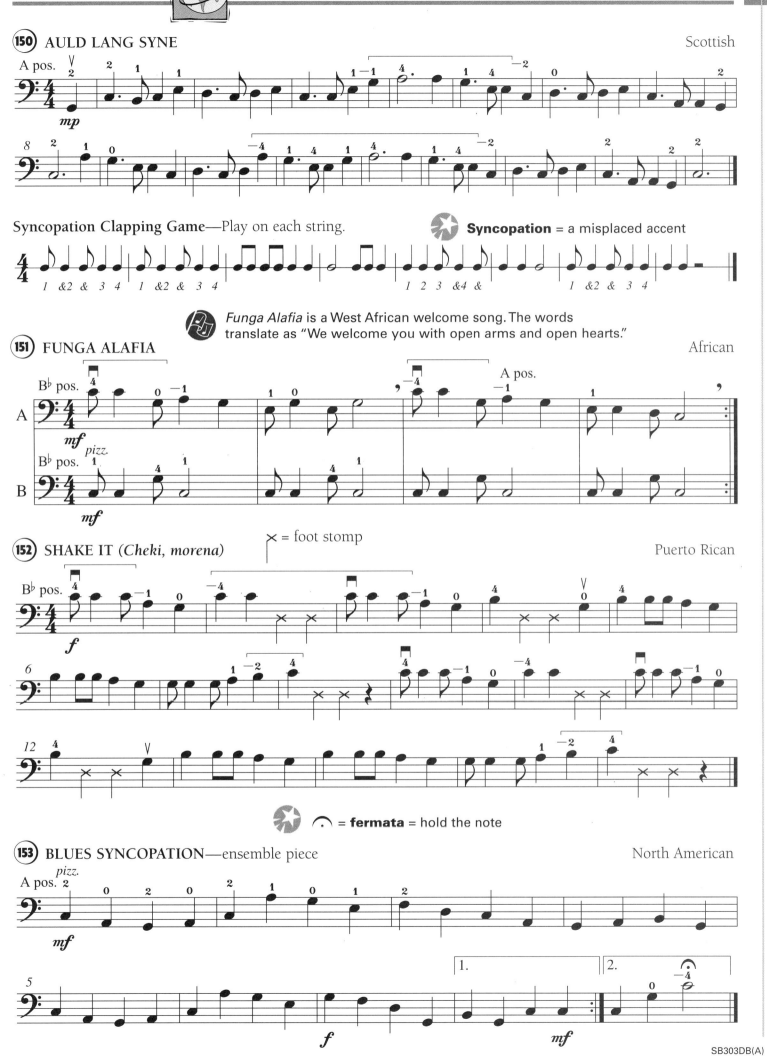

154 MI GALLO (Round)

Mexican

Cripple Creek is a fiddle tune from the southern United States. It may originally have been played on the banjo.

155 CRIPPLE CREEK

North American

The minuet is a graceful dance in a meter of three. This minuet was written by J.S. Bach (1685–1750) for the *Harpsichord Suite in g minor.* Bach was a composer and organist from a very musical German family.

156 MINUET NO. 1

Johann Sebastian Bach

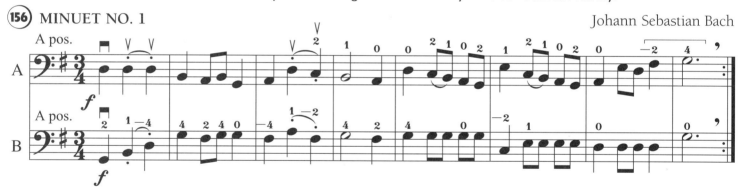

Gioachino Rossini (1792–1868) was an Italian composer. Very famous in his own time, he played viola, French horn, and sang. His opera, *William Tell,* was first performed in 1829.

157 WILLIAM TELL—ensemble piece

Gioachino Rossini

Double Stop March

 Double stop = playing two strings at the same time

Elliot Del Borgo

Bagpipes and Kilts

Soon Hee Newbold

Rock-on Strings

Soon Hee Newbold

Arpeggio = notes of a chord played separately

D Major Scale and Arpeggio

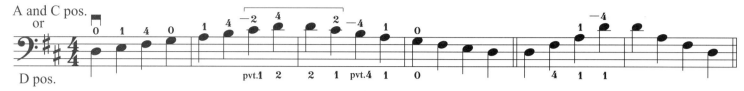

161 CALISTHENICS IN D

162 ADVANCED MUSICIANSHIP STUDY IN D

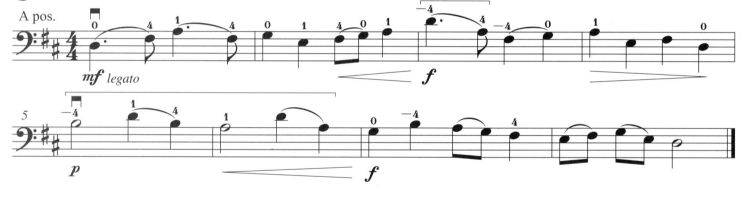

G Major Scale and Arpeggio

163 CALISTHENICS IN G

Memorize One of These Solos

173 LAVENDER'S BLUE

181 Piano Accompaniment Only

English Folk Song
arranged by Kathleen Horvath and Matthew Johnson

Karl Goldmark (1830–1915) was a Hungarian composer. *The Rustic Wedding Symphony,* which opens with this March, features the double basses. Goldmark began his musical studies on violin, and is noted for teaching other famous composers, including Sibelius, composer for *Finlandia.*

174 MARCH

182 Piano Accompaniment Only

Allegro = Lively (♩ = 132)

Karl Goldmark
arranged by Kathleen Horvath

Accent (>) emphatic bow strokes.

Accidentals (♯, ♮, ♭) sharp, natural, and flat symbols for altering pitch.

Arco to play using the bow.

Arpeggio notes of a chord played separately.

Beat the pulse of the music.

Bow lanes point of contact of the bow, near the bridge or near the fingerboard.

Chromatic moving up or down by half steps.

Clef sign (𝄢) located at the beginning of each line of music, the clef sign defines the letter names for the lines and spaces on the staff for your instrument.

Crescendo (———————) gradually playing louder.

Détaché change of bow direction.

Diminuendo (———————) gradually playing softer.

Double stop playing two strings at the same time.

Down bow (⊓) moving bow toward tip.

Duet music in two parts.

Dynamics symbols indicating how loudly or softly to play.

Fermata (⌢) symbol indicating to hold a note longer.

First ending (𝄆 ▬ 𝄇) play this ending the first time through a piece.

Flat (♭) lowers a pitch by ½ step.

Forte (𝆑) play loudly, with a full sound.

Harmony pitches that accompany the melody or tune.

Improvise creating music spontaneously without using written notes.

Key signature identifies notes that are raised or lowered.

Ledger lines (≡) extend the staff with small lines written above or below.

Legato play with smooth bow strokes.

Maestoso majestically.

Measure (▭) the space between barlines.

Melody main tune.

Mezzo medium, as in 𝐦𝐟 medium loud, 𝐦𝐩 medium soft.

Natural (♮) cancels out a sharp or flat that is in the key signature, or a preceding sharp or flat in a measure.

Octave pitch that is eight notes higher or lower and has the same letter name.

Piano (𝐩) play softly.

Pizzicato (*pizz.*) pluck the string with the index finger of the right hand. (+) = pluck the string with the left hand.

Repeat sign (𝄇) go back and play a section of music again.

Retake (ʼ) lift the bow from the string and return to the frog in a circular motion.

Ritardando (*rit.*) gradually getting slower.

Round the same music starting at different times.

Scale tetrachord + tetrachord. A scale begins and ends on the same letter name.

Second ending (𝄇 ▬) play this ending the second time.

Sharp (♯) raises a pitch by ½ step.

Slur (⌒) connecting different pitches on the same bow direction.

Staccato (·) stopped bow stroke.

Staff (≣) 5 lines and 4 spaces, used for writing music.

Syncopation misplaced accent; emphasis is placed "off" the beat.

Tetrachord 4-note pattern of pitches that occurs in alphabetical order (up and down). For example, D-E-F♯-G, G-F♯-E-D.

Theme melody.

Tie marking that connects notes of the same pitch together without a break.

Time signature indicates how many beats are in a measure (top number) and what kind of note gets one beat (bottom number).

Up bow (⋁) moving bow toward frog.

Upbeat note(s) that appear before the first barline. The upbeat is subtracted from the last measure of music.

Variation altered melody.

SB303DB(A)